This is NOT a normal FRENCH book

Learn common French phrases for everyday use and 500 high frequency words

Illustrated and Written by Muriel Lauvige

FRENCH MY WAY

Don't forget...

You can listen to the pronounciation of all the diaolgues and words in this book for free! Visit our website and download the audio - **www.FrenchMyWay.com**

Table des matières

How is this book different?

No boring French grammar here!

This book combines colorful images and short dialogues to teach you what French people really say and helps you use words to finally respond to them.

What you will find are typical situations that people encounter on a daily basis such as:
- ordering at a restaurant
- shopping in a market
- meeting the doctor
- making an appointment over the phone
- chatting with your friendly neighbour

Each chapter includes:
- **a dialogue** between two characters using the present, past and future tenses
- **a list of vocabulary** for each dialogue
- an introduction to each character
- there are also two teaser chapters on using French for **past and future** situations

Happy learning everyone! Vous êtes prêts?

Chapitre 1
Le restaurant

Je voudrais

I would like

un verre de vin rouge
a glass of red wine

une bouteille d'eau plate
a bottle of still water

des frites
French fries

du pain
bread

un chocolat chaud
a hot chocolate

deux boules de glace
two scoops of ice cream

Vous avez choisi?
Are you ready to order?

Je vais prendre le plat du jour.
I will have the special of the day.

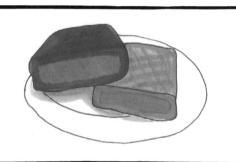

La viande, vous la voulez comment? Saignante, à point ou bien cuite?
How would you like your meat? Rare, medium or well-done?

À point!
Medium!

Et comme boisson?
And what would you like to drink?

De l'eau, s'il vous plaît.
Water please!

Plate ou gazeuse?
Plain or sparkling?

Plate, merci.
Plain water, thanks.

Voilà madame, l'entrecôte à point.
Here you are Miss, a medium steak.

Ça sent bon et ça a l'air bon aussi!
It smells good and looks good too!

Vous prendrez un dessert?
Will you have a dessert?

Deux boules de glace, fraise et chocolat.
Two scoops of ice cream, strawberry and chocolate.

Vous désirez un café?
Will you have coffee?

Non merci, l'addition s'il vous plaît.
No thanks, the bill please.

La cliente

Le serveur

Chapitre 2
Le marché

Donnez-moi

Please give me

un morceau de fromage

a piece of cheese

plus petit

smaller

plus grand

bigger

une barquette de fraises

a box of strawberries

une part de gâteau

a slice of cake

deux cents grammes

Two hundred grams

cinq cents grammes

Five hundred grams

un kilo

One kilo

un petit peu de basilic

a little bit of basil

un peu

a little bit

beaucoup

a lot

une tranche de jambon

a slice of ham

une boîte d'oeufs

a carton of eggs

À qui le tour?
Whose turn is it?

Qu'est-ce qu'il vous faut?
What would you like?

C'est à moi!
It's my turn!

Je voudrais un kilo de pommes.
I would like one kilo of apples.

1 Kilo

Avec ceci?
Anything else?

Une barquette de fraises. Elles sont à combien?
A box of strawberries. How much are they?

Elles sont en promo, deux pour cinq euros.
There is a special, two for five euros.

Très bien, mettez-en deux.
Ok, give me two.

Ce sera tout?
Will that be all?

Je vais aussi prendre des oranges.
I will also take some oranges.

Je vous en mets combien?
How many would you like?

1Kg

1Kg

Mettez-en deux kilos.
Give me two kilos.

Ça fait douze euros.
That will be twelve euros.

Vous n'avez pas la monnaie?
Do you have change?

Non, désolée.
Sorry, I don't have change.

La cliente

Le marchand

Chapitre 3
Les magasins

Vêtements & Chaussures

Je cherche
I am looking for

une chemise
a shirt

à manches longues
a long sleeve shirt

à manches courtes
a short sleeve shirt

C'est
It is

Une jupe
a skirt

trop petit
too small

trop grand
too big

longue
a long skirt

courte
a short skirt

* La taille =
Size for clothes

* La pointure =
Size for shoes

Je fais du 40.
I am a size 40.

Je chausse du 40.
I am a size 40.

Alors, comment ça va?

So, how is it?

Le chemisier me va mais le pantalon est trop petit.

The shirt is ok but the pants are too small.

J'ai le pantalon en taille quarante.

I have the pants in size forty.

TAILLE 40

Size 40

Je peux l'essayer?

Can I try it?

Je vais le chercher. Voilà!

I will go and get them. Here it is!

Est-ce que c'est mieux?
Le chemisier vous va très bien.

Is it better?
The shirt looks very nice on you.

Le pantalon ne me va pas mais je vais prendre le chemisier. Il est en solde?

The pants don't fit but I will take the shirt. Is it on sale?

SOLDES

Oui, il est à moins cinquante pourcent.

Yes, it's fifty percent off.

-50%

La vendeuse

La cliente

Chapitre 4
Au travail

Au bureau
In the office

Je déjeune avec mes collègues.
I am eating lunch with my colleagues.

Je téléphone à un client.
I am calling a client on the phone.

J'écris un email.
I am writing an email.

Je vais au travail
I am going to work

à pied
by foot

à vélo
by bike

Je suis en réunion.
I am in a meeting.

en bus
by bus

en voiture
by car

Salut Sophie, comment ça va aujourd'hui?
Hi Sophie, how are you today?

J'ai beaucoup de travail, mais ça va.
I have a lot of work, but I am ok.

Tu as des projets pour ce midi?
Do you have plans for lunch?

Non, je n'ai rien de prévu.
No, I don't have anything planned.

Julie et moi, on va au café d'en face. Tu veux venir?
Julia and I are going to the coffee shop across the street from the office. Would you like to come?

Oui, super! Vous partez à quelle heure?
Yes, great! What time are you leaving?

On part à midi. On se rejoint dans l'entrée?
We leave at twelve. Shall we meet in the lobby?

Très bien ! Je finis un email. À tout à l'heure!
Great! I will finish an email. See you later!

Ma collègue

Chapitre 5
La santé

J'ai mal

It hurts

au ventre

I have a stomach ache.

à la tête

I have a headache.

à la jambe

My leg hurts.

au bras

My arm hurts.

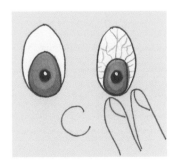

aux yeux

My eyes hurt.

J'ai le nez qui coule.

I have a runny nose.

Bonjour Lucie, alors comment ça va?
Hello Lucie, how are you?

Bonjour docteur Ling, je suis malade.
Hello Doctor Ling, I am sick.

Qu'est-ce que vous avez?
What's the problem?

J'ai de la fièvre et j'ai mal à la gorge.
I have a fever and a sore throat.

Depuis quand?
Since when?

Depuis lundi, j'ai 39°5.
Since Monday, I have had a temperature of 39.5 (celsius).

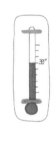

Vous toussez?
Are you coughing?

Je tousse beaucoup et j'ai le nez qui coule. C'est la grippe?
I cough a lot and I have a runny nose. Is it the flu?

Non, vous avez attrapé froid. Je vais vous donner des médicaments. Reposez-vous bien, voilà votre ordonnance.
No, you caught a cold. I will give you medicine. Please rest, here is your prescription.

Merci docteur! J'espère que ça va passer rapidement...
Thanks a lot Doctor! I hope it goes away quickly...

La malade

Je m'appelle Liu Ling.
J'ai 43 ans.
My name is Liu Ling.
I am 43 years old.

Je suis mariée et j'ai
un enfant de 6 ans.
I am married and I have one child
who is 6 years old.

J'aime beaucoup aller au
cinéma le soir ou le weekend.
I like going to the movies
in the evenings or on the weekends.

Je suis d'origine
vietnamienne.
I am of Vietnamese origin.

J'habite dans un
appartement en ville.
I live in an apartment in town.

Je travaille dans un
hôpital à Lille.
I work in an hospital in Lille.

La doctoresse

Chapitre 6
Au téléphone

J'aimerais
I would like

réserver une table pour 2
to reserve a table for 2

prendre rendez-vous
to make an appointment

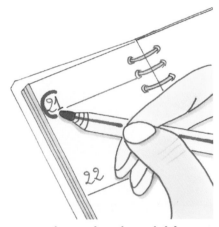

changer la date/ l'heure de mon rendez-vous
to change the date/ the time of my appointment

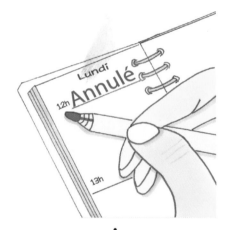

annuler mon rendez-vous
to cancel my appointment

venir plus tôt
to come earlier

venir plus tard
to come later

Salon Bertrand, bonjour!

Bertrand's Hair Salon, Hello!

Bonjour, c'est Annie Blanc. Je voudrais prendre un rendez-vous.

Hello, my name is Annie Blanc. I would like to make an appointment.

Qu'est-ce que vous voulez faire?

What would you like to have done?

Une coupe et une couleur.

A haircut and colour.

Qui s'occupe de vous d'habitude?

Who usually takes care of you?

D'habitude c'est Marc.

Usually it's Marc.

Vous avez de la place samedi matin?

Would you have room on Saturday morning?

Désolé, c'est complet. Il y a de la place l'après-midi à quatorze heures.

Sorry, it's full. We have an appointment available in the afternoon at 2:00 pm.

D'accord, quatorze heures c'est parfait.

Ok, 2:00 pm is perfect.

C'est noté! Quel est votre numéro de téléphone?

Very well! What is your phone number?

Mon numéro de portable est le 06 12 34 76 28.

My cell phone number is 06 12 34 76 28.

Merci, à samedi.

Thank you, see you on Saturday.

Je m'appelle Annie.
My name is Annie.
Je suis belge, mais j'habite en France.
I am from Belgium, but I live in France.
J'ai déménagé en 1990.
I moved in 1990.
Je suis divorcée et j'ai un fils qui a 20 ans.
I am divorced and I have a son who is 20 years old.
J'aime aller au restaurant et cuisiner pour mes amis.
I like to go to restaurants and cook for my friends.
Je travaille chez Air France.
I work at Air France.

La cliente

Le coiffeur

Chapitre 7
Dans la rue

Allez
Go

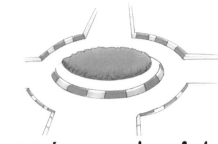

Jusqu'au rond-point

until the roundabout

Jusqu'au feu rouge

until the traffic light

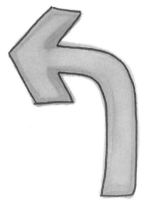

à gauche

to the left

tout droit

straight

à droite

to the right

devant la pharmacie

in front of the pharmacy

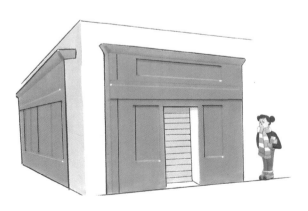

à côté de la pharmacie

next to the pharmacy

Bonjour, excusez-moi, je cherche la gare.

Hello, excuse-me, I am looking for the train station.

Bonjour, vous êtes à pied ou en voiture?

Hello, are you walking or going by car?

Je suis à pied, c'est loin d'ici?

I am walking, is it far from here?

Non c'est à cinq minutes.

No, it's a five minute walk.

Vous prenez la deuxième à gauche au feu.

Take the second left after the traffic light.

Vous pouvez répéter s'il vous plaît?

Could you repeat this please?

Vous tournez à gauche après le feu.

Turn left after the light.

Après le feu, je tourne à gauche c'est ça?

After the light, I turn left, is that right?

C'est ça, ce n'est pas loin.

Yes, it's not far.

Merci beaucoup, c'est très gentil. Bonne journée!

Thanks a lot, it's very nice of you, have a good day!

Passez de bonnes vacances à Cannes!

Enjoy your holidays in Cannes!

La touriste

Le week-end
On the weekends

Je vais au cinéma avec des amis.
I am going to the movies with my friends.

Je me repose.
I am resting.

Je travaille sur l'ordinateur.
I am working on my computer.

Je fais du sport.
I am exercising.

Je vais au restaurant avec ma femme/ mon mari.
I am going to the restaurant with my wife/my husband.

Je fais les courses.
I am going grocery shopping.

Salut Marie, tu vas bien? Les jours rallongent, c'est bon pour le moral!

Hi Marie, how are you? The days are getting longer, it lifts your spirits.

Oui, ça va! Il commence à faire chaud, ça fait du bien!

I am good! The weather is getting warmer, it feels good.

Au fait, on organise un apéritif ce soir, tu es libre?

By the way, we are having drinks at home tonight, are you free?

Oui, à quelle heure?

Yes, what time?

Vers 20 heures.

Around 8:00 pm.

20:00

Très bien, je passerai après le travail.

Great, I'll come by after work.

Qu'est-ce-que j'apporte? Du vin?

What should I bring? Some wine?

Du vin, c'est bien.

Wine is good.

Ça marche!

Ok, great!

Vous faites quoi ce week-end?

What are you doing this weekend?

On n'a rien de prévu, on va aller faire un tour avec la petite, et toi?

We don't have anything planned, we will go for a walk with the baby, what about you?

Je pensais aller à la plage. On verra... à tout à l'heure!

I was thinking about going to the beach. We'll see... See you later!

Les voisins

La voisine

Chapitre 9
Le futur

Le futur
The future tense

Il existe deux types de futur:
There are two types of future tenses:

Le futur proche

"Je vais manger équilibré."

"I am going to eat healthy."

Futur proche is used for an action taking place in the immediate future with words like "tonight" or "this weekend". These are actions that are more likely to happen.

Le futur simple

"Nous mangerons au restaurant."

"We will eat at the restaurant."

Futur simple is used for an action taking place later with words like "maybe","one day", "next year", etc... These are actions that are less likely to happen.

Au régime...

Envie de vacances

Chapitre 10
Le passé

Le passé
The past tense

Il existe plusieurs formes de passé, les plus utilisées sont:

There are many types of past tenses,
the most commonly used are:

Le passé composé

"J'ai lu un livre
ce week-end."

"I read a book this weekend."

The "passé composé" is a
past tense expressing a series
of actions completed in the past.

L'imparfait

"Je lisais beaucoup
quand j'étais petite."

"I read a lot when I was young."

The "imparfait" is a descriptive
past tense which indicates an
habitual action or state of being.
It is also used for physical and
emotional descriptions.

La petite fille

Carte de France

Voici quelques-uns des personnages du livre!

Meet some of the characters of the book!

Thank you / Merci!

Having spent more than 15 years teaching French around the world, this book represents my experience with students learning the basics of French and what the hundreds of students taught me along the way.

Many friends have supported me through the "birth" of this book with lots of praise and enthusiasm. I would like to thank them here!

A special merci to my dear husband Vincent, who patiently taught me how to use design softwares to put together my drawings and turn them into this book.

Grazie mille to my art teacher Massimiliano, who helped me to find my own style and spent many afternoons giving me advice and tips.

Finally, a huge thank you to John-Paul, who encouraged me to turn my idea into this book.

Of course, **thank YOU** for being interested in learning French with me! I hope you will have as much fun learning French as I had in making this book!

Muriel Lauvige

That's all for now!

I hope you have enjoyed learning with this comic book. If you have any questions, get in touch via our website and join the "French My Way" community to receive updates on tips and tricks on learning French.

www.FrenchMyWay.com

A Bientôt!

Deuxième édition

ISBN: 978-2-9545565-0-5
Imprimé avec Create Space

Printed in Great Britain
by Amazon